The Laura Nyro That I Knew
Stories from Bandmates and Friends

Compiled by John Stix

Interviews by John Stix

Cover photo by Patty DiLauria

Cover design by Debbie Phillips

Copyright © 2020 John Stix

ISBN: 9798697859964

CONTENTS

INTRODUCTION AND ACKNOWLEDGMENTS

There was a time in the early 2000s when Cherry Lane Music, my employer, worked with the estate of Laura Nyro. The direct result for me was meeting Patty DiLauria, Laura's friend, and keeper of much of Laura's music. Our first project together was titled *Time and Love: The Art and Soul of Laura Nyro*. It included sheet music to 17 songs, unique photos, Laura's handwritten notes and three previously unreleased songs on a CD. Our second book was *Laura Nyro: Lyrics and Reminiscences*. It included all of Laura's lyrics, some of which had never been in print before, stories from those who knew or worked with her, and a disc that contained Laura's audio autobiography. Both of these books are now out of print. While Laura's sheet music is available on line (see sheetmusicdirect.com), I realized the stories that I had collected for *Lyrics and Reminiscences* could have a second life in this book, *The Laura Nyro That I Knew: Stories from Bandmates and Friends*. The first time around I kept the reminiscences concise and limited. Looking back now on my interview notes, I found there were a few more stories to share. So here they are.

Special thanks to:
Patty DiLauria who graciously gave me the cover photo and permission to transcribe the audio portion originally found on the disc included with *Lyrics and Reminiscences*. With luck we'll do a fourth book together.

Mark Phillips, the original music editor of *Time and Love: The Art and Soul of Laura Nyro*, who knows how to bring music and books to life.

Hal Leonard Corporation for green-lighting this book.

LAURA NYRO, ARTIST

Following the diagnosis of her illness, Laura very much wanted to express the meaning of music in her life for posterity. Her partner, Maria, a painter, was to become her videographer.

Maria, devastated by the diagnosis and desperately seeking some helpful course of action for Laura, kept postponing the project feeling that the illness deserved complete attention. Finally—and this was not much later because treatment began quickly—Laura put her foot down. This was what she wanted, she said, and did she have to hire someone to help her with it? It wasn't an entreaty, but an ultimatum.

"Laura always knew what she wanted in life and never more so than when life became ever more precious. The words you [see] here come from that creative collaboration between the poet and the painter."— Patty DiLauria, Laura and Maria's friend

The Laura Nyro monologue included below is a transcription of the audio heard on the disc that came with the original book.

* * * * *

I thought we maybe talk about all these years later, writing and still feeling you know, that creative dance with music.

I haven't totally woken up yet, but when I do you better watch out.

Music was the creative force in my life as a kid. I was very lucky as a kid, because we used to go out at night and sing. And there were harmony groups there, out on the street, in the hallways for that natural echo. I was just very lucky to . . . it was a beautiful life when I was 14, 15, 16, and 17, just going out and singing with the different harmony groups in the city. We used to do that at night. Nothing professional, just that was our life. It was very joyful.

And the music that was happening then was, I think, amazing music. When I was about, I guess, 14, 15, John Coltrane and Miles Davis were happening. Music was just so great. The jazz that was happening. And, ah, you know the doo wop and soul music and even folk music was really happening. So there was like this great cross-section of music that you could tune into and that you did not have to find a special station for it, it was just all over the place, in New York anyway. I don't know, the quality of life was fantastic with that kind of music happening. I've always missed it since then. But I listen to it. Then I'll always have like certain favorite songs that I hear always. All through the years, no matter what's happening. That's what I tune into.

I think songwriting is a really happy profession. I love songwriting and I just want to continue to do it every day.

The writing I was doing at a young age was very influenced by poetry that I was reading, including Chinese poets and very dramatic heartbreaking poetry from the Chinese poets. That's something that I always see now as I read international poets because that keeps me in touch with the world, and with the people in a real way. As opposed to the news, which is just how much negativity can you take?

For me, singing is like flying. It's the closest thing to flying. One of my favorite singers when I was growing up was Mary Wells. And I always listened to Billie Holliday on and off through the years and still do.

As far as singing goes there's a certain jazz sensibility, an approach to phrasing that I really like. There's something that I used to love about the old-time jazz singers, just a certain kind of phrasing. It wasn't about just big pipes. When I was growing up I listened also to Nina Simone a lot. There's a song that I sing now that I first heard her sing. "You Are Too Good to Me" ("He Was Too Good to Me"). It is one of my favorite songs. Nina Simone sang about progressive politics, about love, intimacy, anger; she was a great artist.

To me, songwriting is musical architecture. It's exciting, it's peaceful. It can be frustrating but you just can't let yourself get into that energy. You just have to work every single day. That's how I look at songwriting.

That's why I'm very interested in the arts. Because it's just another way of seeing life that I just think is more exciting. And just kind of integrated spirituality built into having a life with art in it.

As a writer I use everything, Feminism, my spirituality, motherhood. It all colors, the writing that I do. I don't accept any limitations as a writer or in popular music. But just in general the writer's life to me means I can write now whatever I want to and that's a great freedom. I cherish that freedom.

I have great respect for the animal rights movement and a more humane approach to creatures of the earth. It's just a very simple feeling that I have about all this.

I'm just . . . have always been a rebel in society and always will be. I just think things have to be integrated between capital gain and spirituality and I also believe in a society where there is abundant funding for the arts and that really keeps an eye on things as far as, you know, that kids feel safe in their society. And everybody else. I think you can achieve that in society and I think that at times we have had that.

So I'm 47 years old and it's been quite a life. Being Italian, Catholic and Jewish, which I just have to say *Oy Vey Marone.*

ARTIE MOGUL, MUSIC PUBLISHER

It was 1966 in New York. I think we were at Milt Okun's office. Laura must have been 18. She was enormously talented. This was probably our second meeting and we asked her to play some more songs. She was nervous. At one point I wanted to see if she knew anybody else's songs, which I admit, in Laura's biography by Michele Kort, that it was stupid of me to ask. The next step was, I went out and got Jerry Schoenbaum to sign her and we recorded what became *The First Songs* (aka *More Than a New Discovery)* for Verve/Forecast.

MILT OKUN, PRODUCER, *THE FIRST SONGS*

I was hired by her manager and publisher, Artie Mogul and Paul Barry. Mogul was her publisher and Barry was her manager, they split the jobs. They hired me to produce an album. They brought her up to the studio and I listened to her sing and was very taken with her. I think she was 18. I was taken with her voice, I was taken with her lyrics, I was taken with her melodies. I was taken with her singing and piano playing. I didn't realize that the one thing she lacked was organization, the sense of structure of a song.

She would come up to my studio and play songs. She would come up with her mother, who was just a lovely woman. I tried to get her songs into recordable shape. At first Laura wouldn't hear of cutting the songs. She wanted them just as she did them. She would sit at the piano and it was music as a stream of consciousness. Never went anyplace, never got anyplace. But it was very beautiful. I tried to convince her if we could cut the songs and put them into a form that had a beginning, middle and end it would be much more conducive to people listening. I remember her mother, Gilda, was very helpful in trying to convince her to listen. "Laura, the man knows," she said. But Laura was adamant that her vision is the way it was going to be.

I made a breakthrough when I took one of her songs and cut it down from seven minutes to three minutes and did a recording with Peter Paul and Mary of "And When I Die." Before it came out, as soon as I recorded it, I played it for Laura and her mother and Laura said it seems like everything is in there. It works. That was the breakthrough and she began to allow me to edit her somewhat. So each day we made a little more progress and got the songs into shape. Finally, we went into the studio and recorded.

Was it a fast recording?

It was a fast recording. I had a marvelous arranger. I originally was going to arrange it myself, but my problem was Laura really needed hands-on handling during the session. I would not have been able to conduct and do the arrangements and handle her, I thought. I got a wonderful arranger, Herb Bernstein, and he also contributed a bit to tightening the songs. It was not a tough recording.

Were the vocals live?

I think, I wouldn't swear. We recorded her playing the piano and singing and if the piano playing was solid enough, we then added rhythm and the orchestra. That was on some songs; other songs that had big arrangements we did live. She did a live guide recording and worked on it afterwards.

You started *Eli*?

We had done five or six songs for the second album. If I remember, five of them made it onto the second album. Some of those songs were edited in a sense like we did the first album. Most of the album was kind of long songs.

Were any of those songs recorded when you did the first album, or was it another cycle years later?

It was done later. The songs that I worked on we never recorded. It was months of getting the songs into shape. It might be that we did record them, but I don't think they were used. I don't remember.

What do you have to say about her as an artist?

I thought her vocals were beautiful, her phrasing marvelous and she endowed the words with wonderful color. She reminded me in some sense of a great opera singer who colors the notes with the meaning of the words.

She was kind of special, unusual. I was very disappointed when suddenly our work stopped. I literally never spoke to her again. Only 18 months ago was I contacted by her partner who said Laura said I was the only adult who really treated her kindly and with understanding of what she was and who she was. Before that I had felt that Laura was my one failure. I had a number of successes and a large number of records that didn't make it, but I didn't consider them failures. My one failure is Laura because it ended on a sour note. So then when I heard how she felt, I felt very good. The fact they wanted Cherry Lane Music to handle the songs was great.

ALAN BOMSER, LAWYER

Milt had a terrible partner, a bad guy who was in that publishing company. I represented her making the CBS deal and worked with Geffen who had just come out of the mailroom. He had two clients, Laura and the 5th Dimension. He gave all of her songs to the 5th Dimension, who made the hits out of them.

Here is the story about how her publishing company came to be named Tuna Fish Music. She invited me and Geffen to her one-bedroom penthouse apartment on the West Side that she shared with an enormous German shepherd who immediately pinned me to the wall. She pulled him off. She cooked us this chicken dinner that was totally raw and inedible. We told her that we really couldn't eat it. She said, "That's what everybody says, but I really know how to make tuna fish salad." So she made us tuna fish salad. So when it came time to form her company, I called it Tuna Fish Music. Geffen left William Morris, taking her with him and then managed her. At that point I no longer represented her. For a year or so it was wonderful.

HERB BERNSTEIN, ARRANGER,
THE FIRST SONGS

Were you brought in by Milt Okun?

I was working for Bob Crewe at the time. We had a couple of hit records. Things were starting to cook for me. Milt came in and he spoke to Bob. Bob said, "I think your best bet is to work with Herb on this." Bob is a great songwriter and producer, but he wasn't an orchestrator. Bob is an arranger and he felt that Milt needed someone to work with her on the music. Not to write songs. Milt came into the office and we met. It was instant affection. I like his demeanor, that easy-going nature. Laura and I hit it off, and he played me some of the things. I knew they had seen some other people. Laura decided she would like to work with me, which was wonderful. I was really turned on by her sound and some of the songs. I felt she was little bit too artsy-fartsy. For example, on "Wedding Bell Blues" there were a lot of stops and starts, a lot of stuff that would take it out of the commercial vein. I worked with her on that. Milt gave me free reign. He knew I knew what I was doing. That's one thing about Milt, he recognized talent, whether it was Peter, Paul and Mary, or John Denver, or Laura. He knew talent.

Would you take the basic tracks and arrange around that?

No, there were no tracks, no lead sheets; there was nothing. There was Milt Okun standing there, there was Laura, and there was me. She sat at the piano and played me some of the songs. I put a lead sheet together and Milt put the arrangement together. She knew what she wanted. I was sort of the devil's advocate. She had this raw talent, which was wonderful. I just tried to embellish what she was doing.

Truthfully the ideas were hers, I took what she was doing at the piano and put it into a form which was more acceptable then stops and starts, except on tunes like "Lazy Susan" and "I Never Meant to Hurt You," which called for that artsty kind of approach. "Flim Flam Man," "Wedding Bell Blues," "When I Die," "Stoney End," she had that feel. I had to capture on record what she was laying down. It was tricky because I didn't want to bastardize what she was doing. I just had a hit with Norma Tanega, who was strictly a folk artist. I took a tune of hers called "Walking My Cat Named Dog" and turned it into a very commercial record. We sold 800,000. We had a hit record. A lot of people criticized me that I bastardized her thing. Like I had a Mo-town bass line going. A lot of people were mad at me, those purists. I didn't want to make the same mistake with Laura. I tried to keep the wonderful stuff she was doing and not let it get too off the path.

Do you have any anecdotes about working with her?

I remember once we were working on songs. She said, "I have a whole gourmet meal for you. You're going to love it." I said, "That's great, I'm starving." She came out with this little platter of tuna fish or chicken salad and some old tomatoes that looked like they were out on the street. Some iced tea and she had no sugar. It was the worst. I said, "Laura let's take a little break and I'll buy you lunch." This was her gourmet preparation and it was the worst lunch I ever had.

I lost touch with her in later years. She played the Bottom Line and I went to see her. I went backstage. I wanted to cry. She kissed my fingers. She said, "Oh you genius, I love you." It was so nice, I can't tell you.

Did you work on *Eli*?

I started the second album and I did "Stoned Soul Picnic," "Lu," a couple of others. What happened was, there was a problem between Milt and [record company executives] Artie Mogull and Paul Barry, and David Geffen came into the picture. What happened was, David said I bastardized her songs, the very thing I was trying to avoid. That she should do her artsy-fartsy thing. I credit Artie Mogull too with "Wedding Bell Blues." He had some good ideas there. Milt knew when to open his mouth and when to let me run with it. That was great. I like doing my own thing. I always had a hard time working with people who felt they had to sit on me and tell me what to do. When she parted with them she parted with me as well. She went to Charlie Calello. Which is interesting because she had seen Charlie Calello before she saw me for the first album, and decided to go with me. People were giving her a lot of advice. When you are cooking all of a sudden, everyone has advice and everyone knows what you should be doing.

Do you have any favorite songs or performances on the first album?

When MGM gave us the budget, it was not a big budget at all. I could use some strings on three or four sides. If you listen to that album, there are four men, five men, three men. What it forced me to do is be really creative and go in with piano, bass and drums. I went in with Toots Thielemans on harmonica, Jay Berliner on guitar and Stan Free on piano. I use an alto sax, bass flute, and a cello. On "Billy's Blues" I used a bluesy trumpet thing right out of a smoky nightclub. This is something no one knows. Maybe Milt. When we mixed "Billy's Blues," at the end there is a chime. I love it. The chime fades. When they cut the tape or pressed the album they cut that chime off. When they tightened it up they eliminated that chime. Every time I hear that I get so mad. That chime should be at the end of that song. Whenever I hear it I go, where is that goddamn chime?

What about a favorite performance?

I loved "Lazy Susan." I love "I Never Meant to Hurt You." Laura had something. I guess it's heart. There are a lot of singers that sing better than she did or sing great. It was a heart, a soul, a little waif of a girl, lost, doing stuff she shouldn't do. Laura was off the wall, but a loving off the wall, not dangerous, except to herself. I can't believe she is gone at such a young age.

Because you had a limited time you had to be creative. Was there a model you used for the record?

Peggy Lee's album *Black Coffee*. I still love that album. It's simple, it's creative. Even though it's just a small group, a trio, maybe a quartet on some, it was so creative. That they did it all artistically without having the orchestra. When I had the limited budget on Laura's album, I was forced to be creative. I was thinking of *Black Coffee* and I threw in a cello, a bass flute, a Toots Thielemans on harmonica.

CHARLIE CALELLO, PRODUCER,
ELI AND THE THIRTEENTH CONFESSION

How did you first become involved with Laura Nyro?

When she was getting ready to record her first record, I was called by Milt Okun, I believe. I took a meeting to go and record her. At that point, in the '60s, I had a lot of hit pop records, for them to try to contact me. I heard some of the songs. Unfortunately, I had scheduled a bunch of things that conflicted with her schedule. But when I heard the songs, I felt she was brilliant and was sort of disappointed that they wanted to record at that particular time, and I couldn't do it. But I did meet with them and became aware of who Laura was.

Then when I heard the record on the radio, I found out that the fellow who had then been working with them [Herb Bernstein] had, I think, been working with Bob Crewe at that time. I had started working with Bob Crewe doing Four Seasons records and also doing Bob's early records. After I started to produce records, Bob sort of felt that I was being disloyal or unfaithful. He started to use other people. I think he used Herb Bernstein. I think as a result of that, Herb wound up doing Laura. That's when I first became introduced to Laura Nyro.

The first time I actually met her I was working at Columbia records as a staff producer. Up to that point I had produced "The Name Game," "Lover's Concerto" and Lou Christie's "Lightning Strikes." I had done all the Four Seasons records up to that point. In 1966 I went to work for CBS and 1969 is when I recorded Laura's *Eli* album. After being at Columbia for over a year and a half I went to Clive [Davis] and he says, "I just signed Laura Nyro and I'm going to put you together with manager David Geffen."

So David and I met, and David liked at least my background, that I had the ability to make records with her. David set up a meeting and I

17

went to her apartment one night. She was living at 888 Eighth Ave. I went up to her apartment. She and David were there. She had a one-bedroom apartment, probably no bigger than maybe 15 by 20 feet. It was a very intimate setting. She had candles lit and David wanted me to hear the music.

Laura sat down and played the entire *Eli* album for me on the piano from beginning to end. This is my first introduction. Try to imagine this, myself, Laura and David Geffen in a room with candles and Laura at this piano which was slightly out of tune. She performed this brilliantly. So at the end of "The Confession," when she finished, I was in tears. I was so emotionally taken by what I had heard and realized I had the opportunity to be involved. I knew I could make that record. I was so overcome with having been exposed to this. This is really what I was looking for, to be able to use what I was bringing to the table. So David and I spoke and we hit it off.

He went back to Clive and said he wanted me to do it as a staff producer at Columbia. The first thing I did was meet with Laura to find out how she wanted to make this record. Laura was in her own space. What I saw was that she was oblivious to what went on in the world. I'm not talking about the sensitivity of starving kids or crime and injustice but she was basically oblivious to what went on when it came time to certain aspects of life. So when you spoke to her about music there would be a little gleam in her eye and she would go off into space. It's hard to explain or put it into words but whenever I would see Laura do this I know that she was into a fantasy. There was sort of a childish glow about her when trying to answer whatever question I presented to her. Like, "Laura how do you hear this?" You could see the sparkle and she would go off into space and you would see her chuckle inside. She would not really know what she wanted it to sound like, although she would say she wanted it to be its own child or some statement that you would have to interpret to try to make some kind of musical sense.

I said to her, "Look, here is what I recommend you do. Let's go into the studio, just you and me and let's record all these songs and put them all down with you singing. So we did that. We went into the studio and in one day she recorded the entire *Eli* album on a piano and someplace in the CBS vault is the entire *Eli* album with Laura singing background vocals and her on a piano. I think if they were to look in the archive they would find that tape, which happens to be in my opinion something they should eventually release. It had none of anything that I was about to do. Just her voice and piano, and she did the background [vocal] parts.

Evidently she had put together a group to work out the background parts. After she put together the group, she realized that she was not getting the results she wanted, so she wound up doing all the background parts on the record herself. She didn't know how she was going to get all the parts down because at that point we didn't have enough tracks. We were only recording four-track. Taking my background making Four Seasons records, where we were sort of the innovators of doing four-track overdubs, I laid out a concept as to how she would be able to do the background vocals without it affecting the overall quality of the record. So what we did was experimented with that and we started the project.

After, I had all of the things recorded that Laura and I would need. I would say, "Laura, I think we should do this song like this," and then I would play her various records. I said, "I don't really have a concept for this that I can play for you. What I'd like to do is make this record in the studio and as we make it you can tell me if you like it or you don't."

Give me an example?

When we started with the record, I knew her background, where she came from. She was into jazz and R&B and many different styles of music. She was an eclectic writer. Perhaps a song she had written would sound like jazz. So I would say, "Listen to this" and play her Art Blakey and the Jazz Messengers. I'd say, "Listen to the instrumentation, this is only trumpet and tenor sax." She would say, "Yeah, this would work."

So when I wrote the arrangement at the beginning of "Lu," she would come in and play her piano style. The introduction actually laid down the actual feeling of what she was going to do. One of the things she did, which was very unique as a musician, was that she played chords differently than anybody else I ever worked with. This is something I learned from her and I used this technique throughout my career. She actually learned how to play by the upper parts of the chords. Most musicians when they play chords would play basic chords. What Laura did to play a Cmaj7 chord was to play a Cmaj9 or a G major chord with the C in the bass. They were very unusual sounding chords. I used that technique on a lot of hit records and no

19

one realized that I got it from Laura. She would play triads but she would play the wrong bass notes, which would make the chords. She would play major 9th chords without the thirds. By doing that it altered the sound of the way she wrote her songs. If you listen to her style, all through her life she played that style. Other composers tried to imitate her and tried to utilize that style. Joni Mitchell worked on it for a long time. Basically they were not able to get the thing emotionally the way she was able to do that.

Getting back to the records I played her ... I showed her a technique on "Eli's Comin' " that I had used in making pop records. I told her when I write this arrangement the horns, the bass and the rhythm are going to create this effect. The rhythm effect that we created on "Eli's Comin' " I took from one of the records I made, which was "The Name Game" by Shirley Ellis. Basically, it was the trombones playing on [beat] 1 and the upbeat of 3 and the other horns playing on 1 and 2 and the upbeat of 3. All those musical things that were put into the mix created the element of "Eli." Laura felt that she would not be able to do the song justice if I did that. So she decided not to play on "Farmer Joe" and "Eli's Comin'." She stood in front of the band and sang live on "Eli's Comin' " We did eventually overdub it, but she sang live and it was a very inspiring session. Of course, in those days we did the horns and rhythm live because we were limited in tracks. I hired musicians that I felt would be able to work with her and understand where she was coming from. Although I wrote the arrangements, I was very sensitive to her likes and dislikes.

Who is on the *Eli* record?

Chet Amsterdam played bass. I hired Chet because he was a very sensitive musician. Hugh McCracken did the record along with a guitar player named Ralph Casale, also a session player at that time. A fellow whose name was Dave Carey was a percussionist. He played vibes and congas. Artie Shroeck played drums on "Eli's Comin' " because I overdubbed the drums on "Eli." Buddy Saltzman, a studio session drummer, played on most of the other cuts. Laura played piano.

We did the tracks like that outside of the couple of dates where we did the horns and the rhythm section all at the same time, like "Lucky" and "Lu." Jack Lewis, a well-known jazz producer, came down to the studio to hear Laura and thought she was a genius. When he heard "Lonely Woman" he said, "Man, she should get Zoot Sims to play saxophone behind it." I was familiar with Zoot's playing, but Zoot at that point was a really well-known tenor player. He had not done a record date in about three years. I brought him into the studio and played him the track. He said, "What do you want me to do, man?" "I just want you to accompany her." Zoot played saxophone on "Lonely Woman" and I explained to Laura what I was going to do and why I was going to do it and why it needed this kind of feeling.

We handpicked each and every thing we were going to do. Now, at the end of the record, David wanted the record finished and Laura was really dragging her feet without knowing if she wanted me to put things on the record. So David removed her from the studio with her saying to me, "You're ruining my music." Then when she came back I had done the flute parts to "Poverty Train." I had put some of the strings on "The Confession" and I was able to finish four songs one night while she wasn't there. It was just sweetening with various instruments, what I would call ear candy. She came back to the studio and she pouted for a while then realized that the record really sounded finished.

One reason this was her finest moment was because there was a time constraint that forced her to focus.

One thing that took place—and I think it's sad for all artists, especially artists like Laura Nyro—when Laura wrote the *Eli* record, she had been about three years between records, so she wrote the best songs she could possibly write while that window was open. Laura had the opportunity to be on her own for about three years and she wrote all these songs. When she wrote these songs she wasn't influenced by anybody. She sat in a little room and was virtually not successful. She had a couple of hit records but in her own mind the window of her ability was still open.

After she finished the *Eli* record and people realized what was on that record, the next thing CBS said was we want another record. So Laura started to write and when she came to my house to play me the material, the only song that I felt was halfway completed was "Captain St. Lucifer." I tried to get her to finish the song. But the powers that be wanted to have a record and they pushed Laura into recording a record and a lot of songs that she recorded were really not finished. They have to take into consideration the kind of composer she was.

She really wrote songs that were all babies and she would put them in an incubator and she would nurse them to health. She didn't have that time period to take these songs and nurse them to health. Take into consideration the first song she wrote was "And When I Die." That and the second song she wrote off her first record were hits, basically major copyrights.

Each writer has a window of opportunity that is available to them when they are prolific and really writing their style. I believe that in many respects artists either have a tendency to start to overindulge themselves or they never really reach a plateau where they reach that degree of satisfaction. That was one case with Laura because although the *Eli* songs that she played for me were completed, every time I worked with her after that she never completed the songs.

Milt told me he had to boil the songs down to their essence because she would keep adding parts and get further from the hook of the song.

In many respects the culprits who were responsible for that were the record companies. They allow the artists to indulge themselves without having specific direction. One of the things I provided when I worked with her, I gave her specific direction. I said, "Laura we're going to do this and this." The reason why I didn't do the *New York Tendaberry* record was because I felt that I didn't want to be a part of her rise and demise.

You are saying she had a three-year time window to home in on the songs for Eli. Then there was a time pressure to record. There is a certain intensity in her performance on this record.

The reason why she never reached it [again] goes back to the starving artist. When she made that record she was broke, she was living in a one room apartment and after a while when David renegotiated her contract; she got two million dollars. With the two million dollars, although I understand she never really took the two million dollars from Columbia, her songs were successful enough for her to make a reasonable living for the rest of her life. So with her being able to support herself and making a living, the need for her to get up every morning and to go in and produce music that would actually be something that she really wanted to do, the motivation factor had gone away. Besides the motivation factor, she had control of what she was going to do. She could hire and fire people. She decided to live out her fantasies within her music.

When I went back and worked with her and did the *Smile* record in 1975, I hadn't worked with her in seven years. What had gone on in her life, she was able to pretty much formulate where she was trying to go with her music. But at that point I felt that she had gotten to the point where she had lost—she didn't have that window anymore. That window had closed to where the prolific part of what she was trying to accomplish had eluded her. Although she would write a decent song every now and then, she probably would have been able to deliver another *Eli* record if she didn't continue to record. Or if she recorded once every ten years.

I'd like you to touch on the song "Sweet Blindness."

When we recorded "Sweet Blindness," we did it the same day we did "Lucky" and "Lu," I believe. "Sweet Blindness" was her actual definition of what it was like to get drunk. What it was like to be blind; in a sense it was sweet in a way that alcohol had a tendency to make you feel. When she wrote the *Eli* record and wrote the various trilogies within it, she wrote these with specific points of view. Although I discussed what the songs were about, in her brain I think they were sort of like impressionistic paintings of experiences rather than actually trying to get them to make sense.

What did you mean by trilogies?

When she played me "Lucky," "Lu" and "Sweet Blindness," she referred to that as a trilogy. Obviously the songs are self-explanatory. She felt like she was in a good place and really blessed. "Lu" was written about one of her loves. "Sweet Blindness" wanted to show her transition to being on this wonderful high going into this other plateau. It was written about alcohol and "Poverty Train" was obviously showing the dark side of drugs. She started to get into her own. This is from my conversations with her.

"Lonely Woman" was her emotional feeling about her own relationships with love. She felt like she was that lonely woman. "Eli's Comin' " was also written about somebody that she was involved with.

"Timer," in my opinion, was the most profound lyric. To this day I can't believe what this lyric actually said about what age does to people. And how she realized that eventually what was going to take place was that she was going to get old. You're going to look at yourself and you're not going to know where it happened. When we discussed it, I took credit for adding one lyric. She said at the end of the song "you're a jigsaw timer"; no one can understand why this happened. When she said "you're a jigsaw timer" I said, "Isn't it God that is the jigsaw? She says, "Oh Charlie, I like that. Charlie, I really like that." That was in the song. Again, she knew the eventuality about what would be happening. Because she looked at life as something that eventually people die.

"Stoned Soul Picnic" is where she eventually got herself. That was also about drugs. "Stoned Soul Picnic" was one of those records where I said, "I really can't explain this to you. I have to make the record in the studio." When I made the record and I put the pieces together in the studio with the congas and acoustic guitar and they way they played, this is something that she totally did not anticipate. She loved the record. If you listen to her original version, she played it all on the piano. All of sudden you're hearing this different kind of feel.

"Emmie" and "Woman's Blues" was again, what she was into. I didn't place too much emphasis on her sexuality at that time. She was sort of bisexual most of her life. She had love and she would talk about woman and woman's problems. Woman related to what she said because she would sort of talk in an abstract way about problems that really affected woman that were really in their own little space. When you start to think about somebody in the late '60s talking about "Woman's Blues" and what she is saying, many kids that came from that sort of drug culture really related what she was talking about. She was basically talking to women who were not going to be of the norm. "Farmer Joe," I enjoyed especially the fact that it was an upbeat kind of thing.

Recording all these 13 songs was like four months of my life of everyday with Laura. If I went into talking about every one of these records and if I played them note by note I can recall each and every incident that took place. It was a marvelous experience in my life.

Is there a song that you felt, or you knew Laura felt, came out really well?

I never looked at them as individual songs or individual cuts. I always looked at it as the *Eli* record.

Was the order of the songs on the record the same from the very beginning?

It's exactly the way she played it for me from the get-go.

Was there a performance she was happy with?

No, because she basically did what she was supposed to do on all the songs. There was nothing on that record that she wanted to redo vocally. One thing I could never understand was how the critics never understood her as a vocalist. I thought she was an incredible singer. It was obvious where her roots were. People remarked that she wasn't a great singer. When you take into consideration some of the people who were her contemporaries, like Dylan, come on.

Would she sing with candles in the room?

Later on she would sing and sit down and hold a guitar. I think that was also something else that bothered me about the record that I made, *Smile*. She had started to play guitar and she wasn't a great guitar player. She wanted to sing and play guitar. I tried to talk her out of it. But by that time she was the boss.

Would you do punches or splice parts?

I don't remember the vocal process outside of the background parts. That we punched in. But she knew these songs so well, I couldn't say let's do that again. She would say, "Charlie, I want to do this again. She basically knew what she wanted to hear when it came time for those performances.

Did the musicians know that *Eli* was special?

Talk to Hugh McCracken. While I was in the control room or conducting, he was actually sitting in the band playing the music. *Sgt. Pepper* came out the same year. He came to me and said, "Charlie, this year there were two records that came out, Laura's and *Sgt. Pepper*. He looked at the Laura Nyro record as a landmark record. He played on it and he recognized its value and would be able to confirm the thoughts that we knew its value right away.

Do you have any anecdotes about her as a person?

I thought Laura was very unusual. She was like a flower that needed to be taken care of delicately. She was into her own space. She was extremely sensitive about things. Not emotionally sensitive, but she paid attention to details. I once asked her, when we were working on a song, what she wanted the song to sound like. She stared out into space and then she stared a little more and a little childish giggle came on her face and she looked at her chair. She said "Charlie, I want it to be like my chair." I looked at the chair. The chair was very plain, it was all wood. You could see the wood grain in it. What she really was trying to explain to me was she wanted the song to be really organic in nature. I'm interpreting what I felt she meant. That it would have acoustic instruments. That it would not be brassy. It would be delicate and cared for and curved in the right places. It was a song on the *Smile* record. I don't remember what the song was. When we went to the studio and she listened back to it, I said, "Laura, does this sound like your chair?" She giggled and said, "Yes, Charlie it sounds like my chair."

The last time I saw her was in the late '80s when she was performing in California. I saw her performing on stage and she was having such a great time. To see the fans and to listen to the way she developed the songs she was performing and how the fans reacted to them was thrilling to see.

Did you know about the perfume in the record?

That drove CBS crazy. She wanted the records to be scented. In order for them to do that they had to shrink wrap them a certain way so that when you open the record, the perfume would come off. David Geffen was one of the ones who indulged her to be able to create these things.

I swear that my record still smells.

I'll tell you something else, on a positive note about David. Laura probably would have never seen the light of day if it wasn't for someone like a David Geffen. David was absolutely obsessed with making her successful. When I met David he was 21. I think he must be about 55 now because I'm going to be 63. He was 21 and I was 29. Laura was 49 when she died; she must have been 23 or 24 when she made this record. David would come into the studio and take a look at Laura and say, "Laura, that dress is hideous, what are you wearing that stupid thing, go home and change it." He was very concerned about her image. She would buy a dress that was four sizes too small but she would wear it because she liked the way it looked. She bought things because she liked them.

This was the '60s. Were there any substances involved?

It was part of the drug age and Laura came in one night with a double joint. She took a joint and rolled it up to where it was like six inches long or she connected two joints together. While I was doing something in the control room, she and the guitar players smoked this joint. We were recording, and I think it was something uptempo because it was moving along pretty good. All of a sudden I heard Laura stop playing and I hear her on the mike go, "Oh Charlie, oh Charlie, I feel the keys on the piano." She stopped playing because she felt the keys under her fingers [laughs] and that was the end of the session. Here we were at CBS in the middle of corporate America and Laura is smoking a joint. I didn't get high through that record.

Would you record during the day or night?

We always recorded at night. We would start at 7:00 and record till one or two in the morning. Once we started the project we worked on it pretty regularly, whenever we could get studio time. Some days we worked in the afternoon. Most of the time, we worked at night. Sometimes we worked from the afternoon on through the evening.

Would she play cover songs?

Sometimes she would. She liked Motown music. Sometimes she

would fool around with the musicians when we were doing something technically. As a whole she was basically a serious kind of person. She was really sort of like a nature person. I think the reason why she became so revered in her life was because of the fact that she had reached a plateau that even though she never reached it again, she had reached a plateau that most people never reached.

How soon after this record was done did you think it was a masterpiece?

I knew it as I was making it. The reason is because as I was finishing the record, I said to David, "Before I play this record I'm going to have a press conference." I had never done this before. I said, "I'm going to call all the trades and all of the papers and we're going to have an unveiling." I finished mixing the record at five in the morning and we had a 10:00 playback session for the press.

This is the first time I think any of them had ever attended anything like that. This was my brainchild. David thought it was a great idea. We had it catered. We had 50 or 60 people from the trades come in. I had enough time to take a shower and change my clothes. I got in front of the group and said, "Ladies and gentleman, I'm glad to have you here today to have the opportunity to listen to what I consider to be a masterpiece. I know all of you are familiar with Laura Nyro and have been wondering when she would put out another record. This morning you are going to be exposed to the new Laura Nyro album, *Eli and the Thirteenth Confession.*

Without saying anything else I said I would like you to sit back, relax and enjoy the next 40 or so minutes. I dimmed the lights in the studio and we played the *Eli* record in the studio. At the end of the record I said, "Each of you will receive a personal copy from Laura. I know this record will be released in the next couple of months, but I wanted you to know that you were here first to hear the birth of this child."

What was funny about it was that it had a major impact on the reviews that came out on the record. From the very beginning the reviews were phenomenal. Of course, they didn't see the cover, the pictures hadn't been completely approved and the concept of the performance hadn't been done. When you finally got the whole package and you saw the detail that went into everything of the record, it was like the first of what the industry was about to turn into. I'll give you the conclusion. David made two million dollars on this record, Laura made two million, Calello got fired. I lost my job for doing the *Eli* record.

Why?

I had gone over budget. Normally records in those days cost about $20,000 and I had spent $36,000 and the record wasn't complete. I think the record ran about $45,000, and back then that was a lot of money to spend on a record. Plus there were administrative problems at the company. When Clive took over the company, he hired a new head of A&R, who immediately fired me. I believe the excuse was I spend too much money making records. My response to the head of Business Affairs when I was questioned on it, I said, "I'm making history; I'm not making a record."

TODD RUNDGREN, ARTIST, FAN
AND PROCUCER

Is your song "Baby Let's Swing" about Laura Nyro?

It was inspired by Laura after I had seen a performance in L.A. This is
when she was still inclined to perform. It was an homage in one way
and sort of a recognition of her evolution into another kind of musician.

**In the lyric you ask, "Where did that magic go?" That magic was
not between you and her.**

It wasn't between me and her in terms of a personal relationship. It
was she was already getting world weary at that point. It was the dif-
ference between that and the Laura that I had been introduced to
through *Eli and the Thirteenth Confession*. I felt some disappoint-
ment. I felt that she was constantly going for one sort of monotonal
emotional pitch. It was a fairly low energy thing. That persisted for
the entire rest of her career and life. In that she felt it was almost em-
barrassing to get to the same level of emotional intensity that she had
on *Eli*.

Did you know her at the time you wrote the song?

Yes, I met her when I was 19. I liked the first record. Then I had
heard *Eli and the Thirteenth Confession* and got obsessed with it. My
manager had a lot of contacts and arranged for me to meet her. I essentially went to her apartment in New York City and met her. She
made tuna fish casserole. In fact, it was the only thing she knew how
to make. It was the reason why her publishing company was called

Tuna Fish Music. That was the first time I met her. Then I met her again some weeks later at her behest. She asked me to come over, and she asked me if I wanted to become a bandleader for her. At the time I was in the Nazz. And as much as the opportunity tortured me, because of my admiration for her, I couldn't just simply leave the band and become the bandleader for Laura Nyro.

You both love soul music

We had some commonality there, although she was much more of a student of that kind of music, whereas for me it was a part of the mix of music that I grew up with. I was just as much interested in the Beatles and what English guitar-oriented bands were doing as I was in what was happening with R&B. That sort of left me as something of a disadvantage. I remember the first time I came over to see her and she tried to get me to sing along or play along with her on these classic R&B tunes. Some of them I just didn't know the words. Also, I was really embarrassed about singing in front of her, singing along with her, even. At the time I wasn't a singer at all. I wrote all the songs but I had resigned myself to just singing backgrounds.

She probably wanted you to sing "Ooo Baby Baby."

That didn't come until later, not for me and not for her either. She recorded it and I recorded it, Linda [Ronstadt] and a bunch of people got around to redoing that tune. That was a song that I was well familiar with because the Nazz had done it almost from the time the band was formed. There were certain songs that even though they were irrelevant to what we were generally trying to do, I insisted on the band learning and performing. There were just certain songs you get fixated on, where you think they have a lot of staying power and have impact when you perform them.

Did you have contact with her over the years?

We didn't keep in touch. As a matter of fact, I saw her play at the Troubadour, the solo show, and that was the inspiration for that song ["Baby Let's Swing"]. I didn't even speak to her that evening. The next time that I spoke to her was just before starting work on *Mother's Spiritual*.

Why were you taken with *Eli*?

Tales of that album are legendary in the music business. Anyone who was paying attention, and who was around at the time, was just stunned by the depth of this record. She was like 20 at the time. It was a kind of music I hadn't heard before in terms of honesty and emotional depth. At the same time there was something about the performance of the music that she later would try and put some distance between herself, and the way those records were done. But the way they were done was, I think, essential to the character of the record. She essentially felt rushed the whole time in terms of making the record, because they had so many musicians, and there was a budget. So in later years she would take what in my mind was an excessive amount of time making a record, to compensate for having been rushed through *Eli and the Thirteenth Confession* in something like a matter of days. But that, I think, was one of the things that made the album so remarkable. It had the underlining emotional tension to the point of hysteria. That really gave the album its weight, and on top of it, the songwriting was incredible.

When you don't have a lot of time you can be nothing but honest.

That's it. She was kind of forced to immerse herself in performance a bit more then if she had been given all the time in the world to just do it whenever it came out. Because of the success of that album she did gain greater freedom, but on no record that she made after that did she achieve the same sort of level of intensity.

Hoist by your own petard.

In a certain sense. This is something that as a producer I've learned as the years have gone on. The luxury of time in the studio sometimes is not a good thing for certain musicians. Unless they are under a certain kind of pressure, emotional tension goes out of what they do.

Was there a particular song on *Eli* that got to you?

No, I heard the album before any of the covers came out. I listened to it end to end and it was, to me, it was a whole cloth experience. It was not a bunch of songs. It was an opera in some ways.

Do you have any stories from working with her?

Sometimes you have an artist that has a great amount of influence and impact on you, particularly in your formative years. One of the disappointments, for me, as a producer and musician, is the sort of loss of the magical experience. When you actually do meet the person and start working with them, it's not that it becomes everyday, but you have to operate on a different level.

You produced *Mother's Spiritual*.

She had been working on the record for a couple of years, maybe, and had gone back to all the other people that had helped her before, like Roy Halee. Still she could not get started. She was recording in her house in Connecticut. She had just gotten the room that she turned into a reverb chamber, and new echo chamber, and all this new equipment all installed but no momentum at all in terms of recording a record.

She had called everyone and finally called me and asked if I would just come down and listen to what she was doing, and see if I could help kick-start the project. That being my specialty, that's essentially what I did. I just schmoozed until she finally got on a performance roll, and performed the record. Having said that, I was still perturbed by that same thing, which is she had now achieved the exact opposite of *Eli and the Thirteent Confession*.

In terms of performance, it was a sort of black hole that sucked everything in, instead of energy coming out. I thought the writing was just as good, although it began to take on this other agenda after a while.

When I first met her, she was still ostensibly heterosexual, and by the time she got to *Mother's Spritual,* she was militantly feminist and somewhat militantly lesbian. In that I found myself being made fun of often, just being a man. During the course of the sessions she would have her whole coven come over and they would sort of be like them and me, and me and the engineers, and we would sort of have to cower in the studio while they were there.

The other problem was she was having an affair with a musician, a percussionist who she insisted play on the record. And the percussion-

ist had terrible time. We would lose take after take because of the terrible time of the percussionist. But the subject would never come up, that would say, okay, fire your girl friend and hire a real percussionist. That was never going to happen.

So there were all these compromises to what I felt could have been a much more exciting record. A record that might have had some impact on the trajectory of her career, which pretty much hit a downward slope right after *Eli,* and never recovered from that. Having said that, I thought there were some terrific songs on the record. The first one she sent me, the one she was having trouble with and the one that I really got attached to was "To a Child." That was the first song we worked on. When I heard it I had a vision of how I thought it should or could come out. I kind of prodded her just to get some takes and get an approach on it. Once we got something, she got equivocally satisfied with it.

The idea of full satisfaction was never an aspect of the recording process when I was involved. We would do take after take after take without any judgment being made about any of them. She would say, uummm, that's a nice one. Let's do it again. Which meant that you would have to listen to take after take afterwards, just to narrow it down to what you would want, before you even started the overdubbing process, which was equally torturous. But by then I was extracting myself from the process.

Once she developed some momentum, I was having less and less day-to-day effect on things. She would make all the decisions autonomously and if I would hear a take that I thought was great she would still want to do more. Often because the take would have too much excitement in it [laughs]. It didn't have that properly-under-control thing.

It was very strange in a sense because on one hand she was trying to do something that was very feminist in a way, but at the same time had this almost anal throttle over any inappropriate emotional expression. Which would be more the way a guy would approach it [laughs]. While she was kind of doing what was supposed to be a message in a way, at the same time she was consciously keeping the emotional intensity very subdued. Eventually, the monolithic flatness of it got to me and I felt that I just wasn't contributing anymore.

Are you mentioned on the album?

Since I didn't even finish, I felt behooved not to. I got paid a little bit of money, I think for the time that I put in, which was about a month or so. But once the basics got done I left it to the engineer that I had brought in to finish it off. He pretty much did everything by her instructions from then on. I don't even think I was credited. I didn't really care because it wasn't turning out the way I'd envisioned it or the way I would have—if I had the power of the producership—the way I would have the record go.

That song ["To A child"] was great and there were other really good songs on it. But again, you could fall asleep listening to the record by the time you got to the end. She was just beyond dealing with it at that point. She had so many attitudes about so many things, there was no way to say, okay, do it for us old times fans or whatever. She was very agenda driven. But the agenda was one that was very hard to sell.

ROSCOE HARRING, LAURA'S SOUND ENGINEER, ROAD MANAGER

I met Laura through her first manager, who was Richard Chiaro. Of course, she had a couple before him, when she was 17 or 18. I didn't get to know her until she was about 19. David Geffen managed her before Richard did, and I think there was one other fellow. Rich introduced me to her as a sound person. She needed a sound person and I was that guy. My first sound gig was with the Lovin' Spoonful. Before that I played in a band and was always in the music business.

What was your first impression of her?

I had never met anybody with perfect pitch, someone that could tell you what note you were singing. Although she wasn't a great keyboard player, she had perfect pitch. It was pretty amazing. She was a wonderful musical person. She had rhythm and was very clear on what she wanted.

What album was she touring with?

I think *Eli*. She didn't really tour around an album. I don't think she toured a whole lot. It wasn't like that with her. She would rather write songs and stay at home. She didn't like touring. She enjoyed performing. People at the Bottom Line will attest to that. That's where her best shows were. She played there lots.

You became her manager and road manager.

I was everything at certain times. I was her manager at a certain time, I was her record producer at a certain time, I was her road manager.

First I was her sound person. We were mainly friends. I was probably the only person besides Don DeVito, in the music business, that she liked. She didn't like the music business very much. She liked Pete Pryor; he is a lawyer. She was unto herself in who she picked as her friends. One of her best friends, Annie lived down in the projects of lower Manhattan. I'd drop her off there a lot and she would hang out with Annie and Charles, an interracial couple that were very lovely people. They named their daughter Laura.

Was she fond of her own songs?

She loved them. How could she not. She wrote some lovely lines, some magical thoughts, and she had the gift, that little gift.

Was there a song or songs that she liked?

Mother's Spiritual I think was her favorite record. She was very close with her mother and her mother died of ovarian cancer at the same age that Laura did, 49. I think she enjoyed making it. We had built her a studio in her house in Connecticut. Although she was a city person, after she got to be 30 or 35, she never liked going into the city as much anymore, except to eat. The recording studio scene was really a drag for her. So we built a studio in her house in Danbury and it was beautiful. At the time it was state of the art; 48 tracks, and all the musicians came up there. Some good guys came up there, including John Sebastian, Todd Rundgren and Felix Cavaliere, who lived in Danbury. Will Lee came up and played bass a lot. We had some good times in that studio and that's where *Mother's Spiritual* was made. I think *Nested* was made there too. I'm not sure.

She enjoyed that environment.

She loved that environment. She would just go into the studio and noodle around and come up with stuff. She would call them fragments. She would have 100 fragments that she would make into maybe five songs. Just put them all together in different ways. She was good that way. The songs on *Mother's Spiritual* are really good.

I heard you have a great story about the Schaefer Music Festival.

She was very naive to the whole performing scene, as that story about the Schaefer Music Festival would attest. She thought you could lower the stage, which probably took three days to put up to this 12-foot height. But she couldn't see the first one or two rows from behind the piano. After a lot of discussion about lowering the stage, she came up with the brilliant idea, asking, "Roscoe, could we raise the audience?" [Concert promoter] Ron Delsner was in on that joke. He'd remember that too.

What songs did she listen too?

She loved the Chiffons. She would listen to less than you would think. She never listened to a lot of radio at all. When she would go into the camper, she would have a few cassettes. She loved old rock and roll, the doo-wop stuff. She did that when she was young on the streets in the Bronx.

Did she do backup singing for records?

That's when she was 17 or 18; I never heard her talk about it. She would rather play herself. She was very fond of Yamaha for putting out little keyboards that you could put on your lap. They sounded really terrible but she liked them. They had two or three octaves and weighed about eight pounds. She would put it on her lap and just noodle. She had perfect pitch. Her brother and her father did piano tuning. They had great ears. Her father was a very good professional trumpet player. Her brother Jan was also a very good musician and had almost perfect pitch. He lives in Ithaca, NY. His last name is Nigro.

Was the band well rehearsed?

Very well rehearsed. We put out a live record *[Season of Lights]*. The one with [vibraphonist] Mike Mainieri on it and Richard Davis played upright bass on that particular one. I got a lot of credit on that record. Then there was another live record *[Live at the Bottom Line]*.

Would Laura enjoy the live performances more than the recorded versions?

No. She had a good time performing live, but I don't think it was her cup of tea. She would prefer in her home studio where she did a lot of good work.

Did she get along with Charlie Calello?

She always liked Charlie Calello. He is a very talented guy. He knew her talent and got the best out of her that anybody did. She did most of those early recordings by herself. It was just her and the piano, and then Charlie got musicians to come in and play over what she did. All those good recordings, it was never done all at once. It's amazing; it's hard to tell. It was just recorded with her and piano and then Artie Shroeck; he played drums. He did a great job with all her tempo changes and slowing down and speeding up. She was one of the first people to do that. It was hardest, of course, on the drummer. He did it very well; he stayed right with her.

What albums are we talking about?

The first three. Whatever ones Artie Shroeck and Charlie Calello worked on; that's how it was done. It would be very difficult to get her to have a performance with a whole bunch of musicians in the room. So he decided to do it with her and the piano and overdub everything else. That is fascinating. I knew her a little bit then.

She had a family thing. The band was family, mixed male and female.

Nydia ["Liberty" Mata] and I and Patty [DiLauria] were the closest. I was certainly her closest male friend. Her brother wasn't around a lot. She and I hung out a lot together.

Did she have other interests besides music?

Eating, definitely eating was like a religion thing for her to sit down and eat a great meal. She and I were the best customers of this Japanese restaurant. The first Japanese restaurant was right under the 59th

Street Bridge on Second Ave. They had sushi before anybody did. She and I were in there at least twice a week.

Is the restaurant still there?

I don't know. I can't think of the name. Patty would know the name. She loved sushi. I remember one story in Japan. We did four concerts in Japan and we were there for 32 days. She loved Japan and the little things she could buy. Her husband David [Bianchini] was with us that particular time. We would do a show and the promoters would have a big dinner after the show. The shows were funny in Japan. We would do a show at five in the afternoon. At seven or eight we would have a big dinner. All the record companies would have two guys for everything you needed done. We had eight or ten people sitting down and we would have course after course of great Japanese food and we'd get done at nine or ten. And at ten they would have an English broadcast on their TV. We would go up to her room; the four of us would be sitting on the floor [manager, husband, sound-guy] and dying after eating so much food and Laura would call up room service and get a tuna fish sandwich.

So many people mention tuna fish.

She would always have a tuna fish sandwich, any time, night or day.

I heard she was a bad cook.

She wasn't a great cook. She put things together very fast. She had her grandfather cook a lot. A lot of take-out. She had a very little kitchen.

Did she sit at a piano because she loved it, or was it work?

It was work. Did it relax her and put her in a different state? Not really. It was work, and she loved to work. It was her dangling participles and her little fragments from here and there and she would try to join them all together. I loved watching her noodle. Occasionally I would play bass with her when she had something she wanted to lay down on several different recorders she had around.

Have you heard *Angel in the Dark?*

I'm very disappointed that those people really screwed her. They put out this record, and what a shame. Did you see the thing on *Sunday Morning*? That was like a commercial. I don't know how those people got away with it. They were swindlers. Laura was a great singer-songwriter but not a very good financial person. She didn't have a whole lot of money. She had enough when she was younger for sure. But through some seedy people that I won't name she didn't end up with a whole lot of money. Those people gave her $10,000 and she went down there [Philadelphia] in a couple of weekends and she just did stuff that eventually she really regretted and tried to buy back and they wouldn't sell it back. It wasn't any originals that she did for them, even though she was good at cover songs.

She owns "Up on the Roof."

Absolutely.

She did a great job on "Let It Be Me."

No kidding. Did [John] Sebastian tell you he played harmonica on a Stevie Wonder tune ["Creepin' "]? She killed that. I can't remember which one; Patty might remember. It almost made it onto a record.

Was she happy with her earlier songs later on?

She was proud of them, but she thought that was a different era in her life. That came out of the streets. When she had money, her lifestyle changed. She had a penthouse on the Hudson River when she was 21 years old. That changes you. It happened to her but she wasn't aware of it. When you are brought up in the Bronx on the streets singing in the subways with Spanish guys, you are funky then. When you hire the best studio guys around in Manhattan, it changes your whole outlook. That affected her and I don't think she realized that too much.

Do you have a favorite song?

I liked "Upstairs by a Chinese Lamp." I thought a lot of the early ones were very good. She could have done better in her 30s and 40s if she would have applied herself. I think she got a little bit spoiled. When she was younger, she spent a lot of time doing it. When she got older she would not spend as much time writing and sitting down and being disciplined. A famous line of hers was "Just one more." She almost had it.

Patty was Laura's best friend over the time I knew her. She loved Patty very much. That's where we sent [Laura's son] Gilly [Bianchini], out in Colorado every summer. Patty lived there 20 years before she came back east and remarried. Patty was her best friend.

PETER GALLWAY, ARTIST, PRODUCER, *TIME AND LOVE: THE MUSIC OF LAURA NYRO* (TRIBUTE ALBUM)

I originally met Laura when I was in the Fifth Avenue Band in 1968 or '69. The Fifth Avenue Band went on to open a lot of shows for her, and she and I became friends. Then I kind of serendipitously wound up being brought in to oversee and produce the tribute record. In those initial years, Laura and I became fairly close friends, and fairly close musical friends. We hung out to a degree and got to trade songs and sing songs that we loved. There was a lot of the two of us at the piano singing "Yes, I'm Ready," which is an old R&B song. We would sing some of the old favorites that she loved, that she wound up doing on *Gonna Take a Miracle*. And some of the songs she wound up doing on the posthumous *Angel in the Dark*. I actually co-produced some of the material with her.

Was there something about her that you found musically inspiring?

Absolutely. *Eli and the Thirteenth Confession* changed my life. That record blew the doors off. The thing about Laura for me was her poetry and her passion and her femininity, her feminism. She was distilling a number of styles that she made her own, including Motown, street-corner doo-wop, jazz, Broadway and a poetic lyric sensibility. I also think that *Eli* was groundbreaking on an arrangement level for a pop record, for those kinds of orchestrations.

Was there a song that hit the mark?

"Stoned Soul Picnic" was a very moving song for me. From the early stuff, "He's a Runner" is a terrifically moving song for me. The record that continues to move me the most, that I think is truly a masterpiece, is *New York Tendaberry*. On that album the song that moves me the most is "You Don't Love Me When I Cry," which opens the CD. To open a record with that song is incredibly courageous. It's groundbreaking. And the arrangement that was used on that song was groundbreaking and the dynamic range of her vocal totally gives me goose bumps to this day.

Do you have any interesting stories about her performing?

I'm going to paraphrase a story that I think is quintessential Laura. Have you come across Roscoe Harring? He was an early member of the Fifth Avenue Band He went on to be a road manager for John Sebastian, Laura's road manager and Laura's manager. He was even a co-producer on the *Smile* record. Roscoe told a story at the service for Laura after her death. This is quintessential Laura. Laura played Wollman Skating Rink in Central Park at what was called the Schaefer Music Festival. She showed up for sound check in the middle of the afternoon. The show was to start at seven. She goes up on the stage and goes, "Oh, my goodness, this is way too high. Roscoe, can you have them lower the stage? It's just too far from the people." Roscoe looks at Laura and in a gentle managerial way, says, "Laura, this festival is running all summer, it's taken weeks to create all this. I just don't think there is any way they can lower the stage." She takes a beat or two and she looks at Roscoe and she says, "Well, can we bring the people up." That is Laura all the way.

GARY KATZ, CO-PRODUCER,
WALK THE DOG & LIGHT THE LIGHT

How did you start working with Laura Nyro?

I've known Laura since 1967, '68. We had a mutual friend in those days and I was just starting in the business. We did some background dates together, the three of us. We were friends then.

What is your memory of working on *Walk the Dog*?

It was a wonderful memory. She is just a fabulous artist, a very good friend. To this minute, I carry around a card she wrote to me during the project. It's just a personal note to me about our friendship and the project we were doing together.

Every moment you are working in the studio with her music, her fingerprints are all over it, her palm prints or footprints. She was highly professional and very comfortable in the studio, although very sensitive about her work and meticulous, something I can relate to. Most of the kind of artists I work with are sort of in that genre. It wasn't foreign to me to work with an artist who was as sensitive about her work as she was. I shared that with her so there was never a conflict.

Every track on there was cut live with the band with her playing, and one or two tracks she sang live. There was one thing done totally live; it was just a piano/voice song.

How did she interact with her musicians?

Fabulously. They had chord charts and when we would do overdubs she had as much sympathy for the musicians as you might expect. Whether she liked everything everyone played or not she was always

45

very appreciative of the work they did. It was a pleasure. There were no down sides to working with Laura other than her very meticulous scrutiny of her own work and what she accepted.

Did you have favorite Laura Nyro songs?

"[And] When I Die" is my favorite. Why does some music hit your soul? I was always a fan.

What did she want from you as a producer?

I think she wanted somebody she trusted for feedback. The kind of work I do and the people that I'm attracted to are highly skilled and don't need babysitting, so to speak. She wanted affirmation of her work from someone she trusted. Plus, I would make suggestions, and between us we would cooperatively make decisions. We dealt with each song totally as a separate entity. Each song, as you can hear on there, from one orchestration to another, they were dealt with totally individually as a song. Laura is the glue that ties them all together.

Did you record in Connecticut?

No, we did it in the city at my studio with [Steely Dan's] Donald [Fagen]. I miss her.

When somebody mentions her name now, what comes to mind?

A wonderfully warm, extraordinarily talented singer, writer, and a friend. For me, every day we would go to the studio it was like meeting your friend on the corner. We'd meet early, have something to eat together. It was like going to the corner and meeting your buddy.

JOHN SEBASTIAN, ARTIST AND FRIEND

We went back quite a way. My road manager was also her road manager, Roscoe Harring. He'll never tell you, but his contribution to Laura's life was enormous. When it was a road manager job he would do it. Also, when she was putting together her studio, or a number of those kind of projects, he did contribute enormous amounts of time and therefore was very dear to her.

Our friendship began as she moved up to Connecticut the first time. That was when we began to see each other as byproducts of being in Roscoe's car. Both of us were frequently. She asked me to come and play on some of her later day recordings. I never had any problems. I've heard people describe Laura's recording technique as bizarre. I thought that she was totally available for me and always clear and also went very much by feel. She was one of those people who wouldn't noodle around endlessly with overdubs. She would take a take, then take another, and she'd go, "I love this one," and that would be it.

Here is a story of Laura, our pal, the character. My wife and I were having her over. She came by and by now we felt like we knew each other forever. I was still surprised when she said, "I think I'd like to take a nap." I said, "Sure, Laura, we've got a guest room up there with a TV and whatever." She said, "No, I think I'd really like to have my nap in your bed." I was so thrown and God bless, my wife, Catherine, goes, "Well, sure, Laura, it's right at the top of the stairs." And Laura had herself a nice little nap and then got up and we went about our business. I considered it a gesture of intimacy and one that I appreciated.

Were you touched by her music?

Certainly, it touched me. She was one of the better writers of our era and we had some good ones. She was writing in the big bull ring, if you will. That is she had hits at the time when the likes of the Beatles and Beach Boys and the big boys were shooting at the charts. So the competition was stiff, not for the fainthearted, and she was right there.

Do you have personal favorite?

"Wedding Bell Blues" I always really liked.

You were on the *Mother's Spiritual* record. How did you get involved?

By that time we were friends. But I also would speculate that it was a decision of getting to try me out because she said, "Hey, I'd love to see how this would sound." I would jump in the car and get over there with a set of harps so I could play something, and then she'd like it and that was how it came out. I also wasn't faint of heart when it came to being a fan of hers. I let her know that if she was going to have a harmonica, I bloody wanted to be the harmonica player.

JIMMY VIVINO, GUITARIST AND LAURA NYRO BANDLEADER

I always preface any conversation I have about Laura, that with all due respect to everyone else I've worked with, Laura Nyro is the only *artist* I've ever worked with. The word *artist* is thrown around. That word should be taken a little more seriously. Laura was an artist above everything, and uncompromisingly so. It was a pleasure to have worked with somebody who every night when we did the live show, it was new. Even though we might have been playing the same songs, the same list, it was great.

Also on the telephone she was the sexiest person I ever talked to in my life. I don't know if you ever spoke with her on the phone. If you have tapes of her speaking you will see what I mean. She could make me do things. When I first met her, she had me come up to her house in Connecticut. There was the big house she turned into a recording studio and there was a little cottage that she lived in, very Spartan, Japanese bed on the floor, piano, her dog Ember, and no TV.

Her only playback system was a child's pink and purple Walkman thing. There was no professional recording equipment where she lived. She had the state of the art studio up the hill. For home listening and working, there was just this toy playback unit, which was great. It had little speakers. It was something you would buy at Kids 'R' Us.

She showed me some ideas she had, so she handed me some notes on a paper plate that started from the center of the plate and she wrote circular, outwards in a spiral towards the edges. So you start in the middle of the plate and find yourself turning this plate as your reading her notes. They were just thoughts about the music, about songs, about what we were going to do. I thought that was inspired.

Working with her was a joy. Of course, when you work with her, everybody has a story. Speak to Will Lee, he had a great story where they were recording on *Nested* or *Mother's Spiritual* and Laura stopped the take and said, "Will, can we work on the bass sound, can you make the bass sound more like this wicker chair?" She always spoke in colors with music, more red, more green, more blue.

There were certain things that the guys in the group couldn't sing, that only the women could sing. We had a very balanced group. We had three men and three women. It was such a great group because of the way she put it together. I questioned a lot of things at first and then understood them. Things like having to have a female bass player or having to have a certain amount of women and a certain amount of men. I never thought in those terms for any other project I approached. But I understood for Laura that was a balance, nature; it was correct, it was right. It's the first time I saw anybody hire in terms of sexual balance, to make the group completely equal. It was important because her music required human relationships in the players.

Are you happy with the *Live at the Bottom Line* record?

They were great performances because they were at the Bottom Line. We had performances at the Mayfair in LA that were equally as great. They are honest. Nothing is fixed or changed. The thing about live performances is the best ones are never taped. When you are conscious of that tape rolling it can change the whole thing. But Laura taped so much during that tour that we forgot we were being taped. I think those are great representations of that band playing that music at that time. I'm very happy with that record. The only thing I'm unhappy about is that it can't be found.

As a fan do you have favorite songs?

I ended up loving "To a Child," which is not a famous song. I loved it every night. "Emmie," of course was great too. I begged to play some of those hits at that point. I don't think Laura particularly cared if she played "Stoned Soul Picnic," but I knew that her audience cared. She was so cool about saying "Okay, we'll do it," but we have to rearrange it. Whatever song was done before, we did new arrangements. That was important to her to keep them fresh. I don't know how Laura felt about the early records. She may have felt they were overproduced. Charlie Calello is one of my favorite arrangers. That's what

I do for a living. I always looked at them differently then she did. I thought all the dressing was great.

Do you have any road anecdotes?

A great thing was when we used to be on the bus, she would always say, "Do you think we could live here?" This is how family oriented she was about the band. Whatever town we were in, it was almost as if she would love it if the whole band just lived in a house and we were a family.

We played at a club called the Strand, in LA, and they had one of those big sort of Vargas girls paintings of a girl riding an airplane, almost totally nude. That was the backdrop of the stage that Laura Nyro was going to play on. She made them cover it up with a big giant cloth. She used to say to me, "Jimmy, do you have to wear leather guitar straps? Don't they make cloth guitar straps? Do you have to wear a leather belt?" Then she looked at my boots. We were on the road and she stops at a mall and buys me five pairs of sneakers. You can wear these red sneakers on stage. No leather.

Did that band record in the studio?

We did record some in the studio. I don't know what happened to the tapes. That band were completely unknown players at that time. Laura and I were working very closely together. I always felt that the project was taken out of our hands. When she finally did make *Walk the Dog & Light the Light*, a lot of stuff that we had recorded was being recorded again for that record. But there's hours and hours of tape. I was partial to our live versions.

Laura Nyro was a big artist for CBS; they certainly didn't want to try a bunch of young guys they didn't know. They went with the old studio players, which is always good. Laura had things in the can, which she had done with [drummer] Bernard Purdie. There's the original version of "Roll of the Ocean" with [drummer] Steve Gadd, [bassist] Chuck Rainey and her on piano and maybe Lenny Castro on percussion. That original version of "Roll of the Ocean," which I have never heard put out, was one of the greatest things I ever heard. We learned how to play it from that version. We never approached the heaviness of that version. I certainly miss the hell out of her. The last time I saw her she was playing solo with some female singers.

The Labelle record *Gonna Take a Miracle* is one of the best cover records ever made.

That's a great record, a classic. For me that's maybe the classic album for her. Laura always talked about singing doo-wop when she was a kid with the guys on the corner in the Bronx. She taught all of us who sang with her so much about singing. Just about blending and men can't sing this, woman sing this, men sing that. Every aspect of her songs were her. My opinion is, she may have been offended by some of the covers of her music. I can say Blood Sweat & Tears' version of "And When I Die" is hokey and it's so deep. She took it back when we did it live. We did it with a mandolin and she had this little keyboard, like a toy keyboard she used to play, this Yamaha thing. She loved the sound.

Is there a song she enjoyed playing most on stage?

She loved playing "Japanese Restaurant." She had fun with that every night. Laura was very careful about putting the show together so that everything was enjoyable. We started with "The Wind" every night. That was her way in. It wasn't like we would change the set list. The set had a life of its own. You couldn't do it out of order. It was complete from front to back, including her encores, which were solos.

Did you have any sound check songs?

We had worked on "Love on a Two-Way Street," maybe she even recorded it. "Heeby-Jeebies" we worked on. It was mostly soul classics. She liked the Delfonics and the Dells. I remember her particularly loving to do "Love on a Two-Way Street." If she liked a song, she could make it her own, which is something very few people can do. How many people thought she wrote some of the covers she did. She owns "Up on the Roof."

NYDIA "LIBERTY" MATA, PERCUSSIONIST WITH LAURA AND WITH HARPBEAT

How did you meet Laura?

I went to school with a friend named Peter Dallas. He and I went to Newtown High School together in Queens. When we were 16 or so we had an ongoing bet who was going to meet Laura first. I used to carry her albums around wherever I went, and wherever I ended up I'd ask if I could play them. Peter was the same way. We had this on-going bet.

In June 1970 Laura played four or five nights at the Fillmore East and Miles Davis was the opening act to Laura. I had tickets to every night and I brought a different friend of mine to every show and I never saw Miles Davis. I could shoot myself for it these days. I had blinders on. All I wanted to know about was Laura Nyro. I didn't go to any other concerts. My partner Ellen and I would hitchhike to Jersey, Boston, wherever we had to go to see a Laura Nyro concert. The first night of these shows at the Fillmore, we had already seen the show. By the time she came to New York I knew exactly what her third encore would be.

I always tried to sneak out and get a glimpse of her coming out of the backstage door. I went to the backstage door right before I knew when she would be leaving. Who opens the door but Peter Dallas, my school chum. Of course, I was flabbergasted. There is a beautiful picture of Laura with Peter in the original songbook. She traveled with him all over the world. She met him on the Upper West Side and they became friends and he became her light man. I saw him and said, "You little devil, what are you doing in there?" He told me he had been traveling with Laura and promised me he would introduce me to her. Laura came out a few minutes later and he introduced us. Of course, I was jumping up and down and telling her how I had tickets to every show that week. And that we would see each other again. We didn't get to speak again during that time.

A few months later I saw her in California. I didn't get to speak with her but I saw Peter. They had already gotten in the limo. They were just about pulling off when I noticed that Peter said something to Laura like, there is my friend Nydia and Ellen. She looked out the window and waved to me. We kept running into each other like this, and then I was in California for about six months.

At that point I was ready to come home. I had no money. I was 18 or 19. This was pretty much right before *Gonna Take a Miracle*. I believe Laura was playing at Westbury [NY]. It was in April. I was in California. Long story short, I got this friend of mine who I met out there to fly me back to New York. I said to her I don't have any money but if you fly me home to New York, I promise you, you will meet Laura Nyro. I just had a gut feeling.

When I was a kid, my mission in life was to meet Laura, to play music with her and to be her friend. I had no agenda as to how all this was going to happen. But I was clear. I wish I could be as clear today as to what I want to do. I was clear then.

What songs touched you?

Ellen and I were best friends since seventh grade. When we heard "Emmie," that kind of told a story for us. All her music was so heart-wrenching, so passionate. When you're 16, at that age you know how passionate we girls are. The voice, we were totally taken with the voice and her harmonies. We were always crazy about her background singing.

Sure enough, my friend did fly me to New York. We came in the day before, spent the night in the city. The next day we hitched out to Westbury. I said to her, "I know what we have to do. We have to get there around the time of the sound check." I go to the backstage door. It must have been four or five and I knock on the door and just as we're knocking on the door Laura is coming out with Roscoe, who was her sound man at the time and kind of like her road manager.

Sure enough, when she sees me there with my friend, she recognizes me. I said, "Laura, we just flew in from California. I have no tickets but we had to come and see if we could get in." She told the person at the door, "Please let these ladies into my dressing room." At this point I'm all smiles and nudging my friend with my elbow going, "What did I tell you, kid." So we're in Laura's dressing room. This is as close as I'd gotten to really being around her. All of a sudden people start piling in as it gets close to concert time. Her friends and family. The next thing you know we got seats right in the front and we saw the show.

I didn't see Laura for a little while. Then I started writing notes to Laura and sending her flowers. I knew she lived across the street from the Hayden Planetarium. She had my phone number. One day she called me on a Saturday afternoon and asked me if I was busy. She asked me if I had ever seen the movie *Black Orpheus*? She loved that movie. I told her I had never seen it. I had mentioned the Afro-Cuban religion [Santeria] with the drums and voodoo and all this stuff. Laura said, "There is a lot of that going on in the movie, the Brazilian end of it." So she calls me up on a Saturday afternoon and asked me if I wanted to go to the movies. I was flabbergasted. You can imagine. I said, "Yeah, I think I can do that."

I went to Laura's house and it's just she and I. We were eating tuna fish on Saltine crackers when the phone rang. It was Vicki Wickham, manager of Labelle, and Laura was telling me she was going to be doing an oldies album to pay homage to her roots. That was the music that she grew up listening to. Patti LaBelle and the Bluebells were one of her favorite vocal groups at the time. She was telling me how she was trying to meet them so they could possibly do this record *Gonna Take a Miracle* together. Vicki said to Laura, "Patti and the girls are all available this afternoon and would love to get together with you. Would it be okay to come over?" Of course Laura was thrilled. Now she felt [about them] like I felt about her. Laura gets off the phone and says, "Nydia, would you mind if we didn't go to the movies? Vicky is bringing Patti LaBelle and Sarah Dash and Nona Hendryx over." I said, "No, I don't think I would mind." This is when "Lady Marmalade" was already at its peak. Labelle was very big at that point. I was at the right place at the right time.

The girls come in smelling of musk. They talked a little bit. She told them her idea about doing *Gonna Take a Miracle* and Laura sat down at the piano and started playing "Nowhere to Run," "Jimmy Mack." She played a bunch of oldies. The girls started to sing with her. What we did on the record is pretty much how they sang it right from the get-go. I remember it sounding very similar to the first time they sang together.

Then there is little old me. Laura was not one for clutter and a lot of stuff. I'm looking around . . . what can I possibly use to play something? I spied this little Chinese drum that I have to this day. I started playing a little drum along with her and the girls. They left and she was in seventh heaven and I was beyond. I had told her I was a musician.

As a kid, I knew I was a drummer when I was, like, eight. I grew up listening to rock 'n' roll. Even though I'm Cuban, my love was the drum set, because I wanted to play rock 'n' roll. But I knew that I wasn't quite that good to get on a drum set and go into the recording studio, although Laura did take me into a studio at one point to try to play on "Spanish Harlem." But I was just too nervous. I couldn't pull that one off. So she asked me what I could play and I told her I could play conga drum. Being Cuban, I had played conga drums at parties. But I didn't own one. The next thing I knew, she said, "That's very interesting." I guess Laura felt the connection, since I was there right from the get-go. The next thing I know she's got a concert in Japan, shortly after that.

A couple weeks later I get a call from Richard Chiaro, who was her manager at the time. Richard asked me if I was going to be around that summer because Laura was interested in using me in the recording studio to record *Gonna Take A Miracle*. I said, "Yeah, I think I can manage that." So I went to Philadelphia with Peter Dallas, he and I took the train out there together. [Writers-producers Kenny] Gamble and [Leon] Huff had a band and they had a percussionist. Laura wanted me to play conga. I told her I could play conga; meanwhile, I didn't even know how to tune a conga. So Larry Washington, who was the other percussionist on the record, he ended up playing bongos and I played congas. If you listen to the record you can pretty much hear that the conga is way back in there somewhere; it sounds like a big rumble to me.

Were you a musician before this, or was it just right-time-right-place, I-might-as-well-go-for-it-because-I'm-there?

I was always a musician but I hadn't done anything professionally. There was no doubt I was a musician; I never wanted to do anything else. I knew I would play music and I did play. If I went to a club and there was a set of drums there, I would eventually get on the drums and play. I had little groups, but at 19 I was all for being a hippy, going to California, and following Laura Nyro. I had a job with the phone company. That was the only straight job I remember ever having. After I was a phone operator, I saved some money and that's when we went to California. When I came back from that California trip is when I met Laura and this whole thing happened.

Very shortly after I did *Gonna Take a Miracle*, I got a call from a group called Isis, which at the time was being put together. Isis was an all-girl band. Originally the woman from Isis were Goldie and the Gingerbreads, who were Genya Ravan from Ten Wheel Drive and Carol MacDonald and Ginger Bianco. These women were a lot older than me at the time. They had toured in Europe as Goldie and the Gingerbreads. They were pretty seasoned as far as doing their thing. I had no idea how they heard about me. They called me and the next thing I knew I stayed with Isis up until 1976, when Laura called me again to go on tour with *Season of Lights*. That's when I left the group. At that point I hadn't done anything professional.

My first professional show was during the recording session of *Gonna Take a Miracle*. Laura had a concert, and I think it was in Chicago at an outdoor theatre. She asked me what I thought of the idea of taking Patti and the girls to the show with her. I said of course, that would be incredible. It would be Laura on piano and the girls singing backup. She asked me if I would like to play. I was so innocent. I was too stupid to be nervous. Next thing I knew, here we all were in Chicago, and as I remember it, there was Laura's baby grand and they had rented a conga for me. I didn't even own a conga at that point. There was a stool there for me. I came out first, Patti and the girls came out behind me and Laura came out last. I should have been a nervous wreck but I wasn't. This was during the record. The rest is history.

No doubt that Laura gave me my break in the music business. She was about 23; I was 19 when we recorded *Gonna Take a Miracle*. No matter what I do from this point on, the peak of my career was working with Laura Nyro. I played Carnegie Hall with Laura.

Was *Miracle* recorded quickly?

From what I remember it was done pretty quickly.

Were these songs she enjoyed or played?

She loved Dionne Warwick. She used to sing "Walk On By." I remember her being compared to Dionne Warwick. She loved Dionne Warwick's voice. She liked Aretha [Franklin] very much.

Was Laura comfortable in the studio?

She was very comfortable in the studio. She had a way of bringing out the best in you. She perceived me as someone who could do some things that other people didn't really get that I was able [to do]. I was her production assistant on *Mother's Spiritual*. I can be very scattered, but when it came to working with Laura, I was very focused. She brought that out in me. I didn't realize I could do that and I was very organized. I kept track of all the tracks. She had a way of seeing someone's potential.

Do you have any favorites among her songs?

I think she was very proud of "Broken Rainbow." "To a Child" I think was a classic to her. Of course "And When I Die" she always performed that. She always loved "Wedding Bell Blues." I seem to remember we always did that.

From the few times I toured with Laura, she shied away from the music on *New York Tendaberry*. I think she liked doing the lighter stuff, except "Broken Rainbow," which is very deep, and so is "To a Child."

Laura in the studio would let me experiment on some things, and she would live with it for a while before she made her decision. A lot of times in the studio she would actually conduct my playing. She would show me exactly where she wanted me to play. She would squat down.

I remember when Laura turned her house in Danbury [CT] into a recording studio. She had the whole house rigged so that she could record in any room. We have the conga set up in the laundry room area; not sure why, but that's where we were. I remember her squatting down in front of me and signaling me as to when she wanted a little rhythm and when she wanted me to lay out more.

Why record in different rooms?

You know how in the studio you need isolation booths. We didn't have isolation booths, so she used the house in that way. So this way she could get separation. If she wanted to use a few musicians at a time she could.

Did you have contact with her in the later years?

I was with Laura almost until the end. I helped take care of Laura when she was sick. I was up there from the time she came back to New York. She had her first surgery in California. When she came back I was in Danbury for almost the whole time except the last month when Patty came in. Ellen and I had a prior commitment working with a school in Long Beach. We were putting on a multi-cultural show with the kids. So the last month I had to be here. Patty had flown out a couple of times prior to that.

Was she making music then?

I want to say she was. I would like to say that she never really gave up the dream that she could do it. She was always connected.

Did you hear *Angel in the Dark*?

I'm thrilled that there is more of Laura, but I knew she didn't want to put that record out. The woman who put out that record makes herself sound like a good friend of Laura's. She was not a good friend of Laura. The woman was up in Danbury maybe twice in those six months that I was there. They were not close but this one makes it sound like she was her dear friend and blah-blah-blah, they made this record together. These record companies had turned their back on her pretty much because she wouldn't go out there and promote it the way they would like to see her do it. She had no one who would put out the music. She met this woman and this person offered to lay out some money to help her go into the studio and that's what it was all about. It had nothing to do with what she seems to be saying.

Patty doesn't want me to speak with that woman, so I won't.

I'm thrilled that you're not. She is really nobody and did something that Laura never wanted. Laura wanted to get those tapes before they got into her hands. Unfortunately, because of her illness, she was too busy trying to deal with that. It got put on the back burner. When Maria [Desiderio] tried to get the tapes, they were gone. Laura wanted them destroyed. She did not want to put them out because they were not finished. By the same token, I am thrilled to hear her voice.

I have a record, *Live in Japan*.

I don't know about that. It's Laura at the piano with a vocal group for a few songs.

I think Laura was way ahead of her time in so many ways. I have a picture of Laura when she is 19. As far as I'm concerned she is the originator of what later became known as the granny look with the floppy hats and the black long dresses with the boots. This woman was doing this in the '60s before it was popular.

The other thing she did that was way ahead of her time was eating sushi. I got turned onto sushi when we did *Gonna Take a Miracle*. I wasn't so sure about that sushi in the beginning, but it does grow on you. I love it now.

Laura was kind of a workaholic. When I was assisting her on *Mother's Spiritual,* we would spend 14 hours a day listening to the music that had been recorded. One thing I found interesting about how she worked was that there were times she did a vocal and I heard her voice crack a bit and I would have never used it. Laura didn't care about that kind of thing. She was more interested that the feeling that she wanted to project came across. She was not a perfectionist when it came to sounding absolutely perfect. She was going for something more primal, something more soulful then what I was looking at. I wanted it to sound perfect because I knew she had the voice to make everything sound that way. But Laura didn't do that. She was more interested in a certain feeling that she was going for. I always felt she knew exactly what she wanted, even though she was very interested in people's opinions. She would ask everybody their opinion; ultimately, I always felt she knew exactly what she wanted.

Laura liked simple things. She made great potato salad. She got her fried chicken recipe from Patti LaBelle. One of her favorite things was to have a big pajama party. We'd all go to her house or my mom's apartment. My mother has a tiny studio apartment on 14th Street. We'd all sleep on the floor and have rice and beans and she would be thrilled with that. It would be Laura, Maria, Gil, me, my mother, maybe a couple of dogs. Six of us in a small room and we would watch movies. Her and my mother used to love to watch *Take the Money and Run*. She loved John Candy.

She was a kid at heart. She had the best giggle of anybody I know. There is a very bright spark missing for me in my life. We spent a lot of holidays together. We spent Christmas Eve together a lot. We spent our birthdays together; we became family. My mom used to take care of her son Gil when Laura was on tour. We were very connected. The main thing I miss is her music. But for me, when Laura came to my house or I went to her house it was all about having a good time. There is, like, this bright spark that is not here anymore.

PATTY DILAURIA, FRIEND

Laura told me the album *Mother's Spiritual* was as close as possible to her artistic vision. It was near perfect, ninety-five percent there.

ELLEN URYEVICK, FRIEND,
HARPIST IN HARPBEAT

Laura gave me a harp in 1976. She had been doing her *Season of Lights* tour, and Nydia and I, who had grown up together, met her basically at the same time. I met Laura through Nydia's persistence as a die-hard fan. She got through the wall, and once Laura got to know Nydia, she fell in love with her, and then she fell in love with me. We were all very close from that point on. The year she gave me the harp I think was the second tour we had gone out with her. I used to travel with her also, more or less as a mascot. I didn't do much, but we used to travel together. I was about 24 at the time. I hadn't yet found my calling. I was looking for something. Laura had bought this harp a couple of years before when she was hanging out with Alice Coltrane. Alice played the harp and she encouraged Laura to get one, which she did. They were doing these Swami Satchidananda retreats, where they would hang out a lot together.

The harp is very demanding instrument. It's not the type of instrument you can play around with. You have to get into it or forget it. Laura loved the harp, but never really pursued it that much, although she had taken some lessons. She had to cut her nails, and she didn't like to cut her nails. You can't play the classical harp with nails.

She had this harp in the house and I saw it from time to time when I went up to her place. She lived in the Beresford [211 Central Park West], right near the planetarium. She was in the penthouse and had a beautiful view of the park. I would see this harp up there, and I was enchanted by it, but it was like a Martian to me; it was such a foreign thing. It was beautiful and very foreign. On the *Season of Lights* tour we would talk about what is Ellen going to do with her life. We would get into philosophical conversations. I think it came up a couple of times that I liked the harp or maybe I told Nydia I liked the harp. On Channel 13 I had seen a woman play jazz on the harp with a bass and all the jazz instruments. When I saw that, I said to myself, "If I had a harp, I could do it." I had a feeling that I could play.

When we came back from the tour, Laura was going to be giving up her place at the Beresford and moving lock, stock and barrel to her land in Danbury. She had bought that land from Swami Satchidananda. I wouldn't be surprised if Laura and Alice went to retreats there before Laura bought this land. I don't know why he put it up for sale, but she did end up buying it. It's beautiful land with stones and trees lending themselves to meditation. She bought the land and was living in the city. I guess she realized that she needed to be in one place, and she decided to give up the Beresford.

A couple of days after we came back from the tour, Laura called me up and, in her casual way, she said "I'm moving and I'm trying to prune down. Would you like me to send the harp over?" I was flabbergasted! I said yeah, sounds like a great possibility for me. She said there is no pressure. She wasn't expecting me to become a master. She said just take it and see what you think. I was so ready to bite off something and I was lucky enough.

Would Laura ever just play for you?

She used to play all the time for her friends. She loved to sit down when it was just the family and play for half an hour. She would play some of the old rock 'n' roll songs she never recorded like "O-o-h Child." She would do the older ones; she started in the subways singing songs from the '50s. Those were in her private repertoire. She used to do "Cowboys to Girls" ("I remember when we used to play shoot 'em up, bang, bang, baby.")

Laura loved food. We used to do a lot of eating. She had a big group and a big entourage. It was Jeanie, Ellen, John Tropea and Mike Mainieri; we traveled in this vehicle we called the Green Hornet. It wasn't a mobile home but it had a bathroom and a kitchen. We had a driver called Cubby. One thing I learned from being around her was how to take care of people. She knew how to take care of her friends. Several times when we stayed in one place for a couple of days, she cooked an incredible, Southern fried chicken and potato salad. She cooked it all from scratch in the Green Hornet. It was incredible soul food. I'm not sure about the chicken but the potato salad was a recipe she got from Patti LaBelle. To this day I cook that potato salad. One of the key things was the sweet pickles.

One of the last things she did before she died was go to a dog show. We used to go to Westminster at Madison Square Garden.

PHOEBE SNOW, ARTIST AND FAN

My strongest recollection of her, as for our interaction, was her in-credible generosity with other artists. I had one or two long phone calls with her a few years before her death. She was like, "Are you okay? Do you need anything? Can I give you any help with some-thing, publishing, recording? I have a studio up here (in Connecticut). Do you want to come up here and do some basic tracks?" I was just blown away. I thought we barely knew each other.

Did you choose "Time and Love" to record for the *Time and Love: The Music of Laura Nyro* tribute album?

"Captain for Dark Morning" is my favorite Laura Nyro song. My mother's name was Lily and it was beautiful and haunting. A lot of the stuff that she did was very ethereal like that. I loved her straight-up pop stuff too, but I liked it when she got a little left of center. That song was one of those things that played like a little mantra in your head. I would have preferred to do that. Then they said this is the title cut and we're sort of holding it for the right person. I said, "Let's do a great version of that." That would have been my other choice.

The day I was supposed to fly to LA to promote the *Time and Love* record on a college radio station, I get a call that she had died. I had to go out there and say she had passed away. I go on the air and I'm talking about it and they play a couple of cuts from the compilation record and then some of Laura's stuff. I'm not sure that he had an-nounced by that point that she had passed away. He played a bunch of her stuff and the phones started lighting up. It was young kids calling up saying, "Who is that artist?" "Where can we get her stuff?" As if she was a new artist. That freaked me out. I was like, yeah, absolutely that would be something I would expect.

What would you say about her as a singer?

Looking back to the mid-'60s, when Bob Dylan started to blow up, she was starting to come out with her stuff. That was the soundtrack of a lot of people's lives. People were deciding whether or not they were going to do this. If you listen to her, and you listen to everybody else that is out now, how could she not have been influential to almost anybody? You hear her in so many of the young women that are out there. The first Laura Nyro album I recall having a serious research project with, living with, and schlepping around with me everywhere was *Eli and the Thirteenth Confession*. That's the one I really got emotionally involved with.

Printed in Great Britain
by Amazon

12496957R00041